ᓄᓇᒥ

nunami

Poems from the Arctic

ᓄᓇᒥ

nunami

Poems from the Arctic

Barbara Landry

QUATTRO BOOKS

The publication of _ɒɑᒥ *Nunami* has been generously supported by the
Canada Council for the Arts and the Ontario Arts Council.

 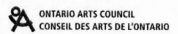

Author's Photograph: Stephen Whitehead
Cover design: Diane Mascherin
Cover photography: Leonard D. Steel
Cover image: detail from the print *Caribou* by Qaqulluk
        Sagiatuq, used with permission of the artist.
Editor: Luciano Iacobelli
Typography: Grey Wolf Typography

Library and Archives Canada Cataloguing in Publication

Landry, Barbara
    Nunami : poems from the Arctic / Barbara Landry.

Issued also in an electronic format.
ISBN 978-1-926802-99-2

    I. Title.

PS8623.A514N86 2012   C811'.6   C2012-901069-3

Published by Quattro Books Inc.
89 Pinewood Avenue
Toronto, Ontario, M6C 2V2
www.quattrobooks.ca

Printed in Canada

for Noah Metuq

Contents

Part III

ᐅᑎᕐᓂᖅ ᐸᵃᓂᖅᑐᒍᑦ *utirniq Panniqtuumut*

Introduction

by Myna Ishulutak

ᑕᑯᔭᕆᐅᓚᐅᖅᓯᒪᔭᕋ ᕙᕗᓚ ᕙᓚᐃ 2011-ᒥ ᓂᖏᐅᒃᑯᑎᓐᓂ. ᑕᑯᔭᕆᐅᕋᒃᑯ ᐃᓄᑦᑎᑑᕋᓯᕖᖕᖑᕐᓂᖓ ᐱᕕᐊᕆᓪᓚᕆᓚᐅᖅᓯᒪᔭᕋ ᐅᐱᒋᓪᓗᒍᓗ. ᓂᕆᐅᓚᐅᖅᓯᒪᖕᖏᑦᑐᖓ ᑕᑯᒐᒃᑯ ᐃᓄᒃᑎᑐᑦ ᑎᑎᕋᖅᑐᖅ ᐊᓪᓛᑦ ᓈᓂᖏᑦ ᐱᑦᑎᐊᖅᓯᒪᓪᓗᑎᒃ. ᐅᕙᓐᓂᓪᓗ ᐊᐱᖅᓱᓕᖅᑐᓂ ᖃᓄᖅ ᐅᖃᖅᑕᐅᑎᐊᓲᖕᒍᒻᒪᖕᒫᖅ ᑭᓯᐃᓐᓇᖅ ᐃᓄᒃᑎᑐᑦ. ᐊᕗᖕᖓᓕᒫᖅ ᐅᖅᑲᖅᑲᑎᒋᔪᓐᓇᑕᕐᔪᐊᕆᔮᓕᓚᐅᖅᓯᒪᔭᕋ. ᐱᖅᑲᓐᓂᕐᓂᖓ ᐃᓄᑦᑎᐊᕙᐅᓂᖓ ᑕᑯᓚᐅᖅᓯᒪᒐᒃᑯ ᐱᓗᐊᑐᒥ ᐃᓕᓴᕋᐃᓐᓂᖓ, ᐃᓕᒍᒪᓂᖓᓗ ᐃᓄᒃᑎᑐᑦ ᖁᕕᐊᒋᓪᓚᕆᓚᐅᖅᓯᒪᔭᕋ. ᐅᖅᑲᐅᓯᕗᑦ ᐱᒻᒪᕆᐅᒻᒪᑦ ᐅᕙᓐᓄᑦ, ᐅᖅᑲᐅᓯᕋ ᐃᓄᒃᑎᑐᑦ ᐃᑉᐱᓐᓂᐊᓂᓐᓂᒃ ᐃᓯᒪᒋᔭᓐᓂᒃ ᐊᓂᐊᑎᕆᑦᑎᐊᓲᖕᒍᕗᖅ ᐃᓄᑦᑑᑐᐊᕈᒪ, ᑐᑭᓯᑎᑦᑎᒐᓯᐊᕐᒐᕆᐊᑐᓇᓂᓗ.

ᑖᓐᓇ ᐅᖃᓕᒫᕐᓂᖅᑕᐃᑦ ᑕᑯᓐᓇᖑᐊᕐᓇᑎᐊᖅᑐᖅ ᖃᓄᓕᒫᖅ ᓲᕐᓗ ᐱᖅᑕᐅᔮᓕᕐᓇᖅᑐᖅ ᑕᕝᕙᖓ ᐱᓗᐊᖅᑐᒥᒃ ᓇᑦᑎᓯᐅᖅᑎᓪᓗᒥᑦ. ᐅᕙᖓᓕ ᖁᕕᐊᒋᓪᓗᒍ ᑭᓯᐊᓂ ᐃᓛᓐᓂᒃᑯᑦ ᖁᐊᖅᓵᕆᓲᕆᒐᒃᑯ ᐅᕝᕙᓗ ᓇᖏᐊᒻᒪᕆᓕᓲᖑᔪᖕᒐ; ᐅᐱᓐᓇᕋᓂ ᓱᒃᑲᔮᒃᑲᐃᓐᓇᓇᖅᖑᑦ ᐅᒥᐊᖅᑐᖅᑐᓂ ᓇᑦᑎᓯᐅᖅᑐᓃᑦᑖᒃ ᐃᓛᓐᓂᑯᓪᓗ ᓱᒃᑲᐃᓕᒃᑲᓪᓚᑦᑐᓂ. ᑖᓐᓇ ᐅᖃᓕᒫᓕᕈᕕᐅᒃ ᑐᑭᓯᒃᑲᓐᓂᓪᓚᕆᓐᓂᐊᖅᑕᐃᑦ ᐊᒻᒪᓗ ᐊᓪᓛᖅᑲᐃ ᑕᕐᕆᔭᖅᑑᔮᕐᓂᐊᖅᑐᑎᑦ ᓇᐃᑦᑑᓕᓗᐊᖅᑎᓪᓗᒋᑦ ᑖᒃᑯᐊ. ᖁᕕᐊᒋᑦᑎᐊᖅᑕᕋ ᐃᓅᓂᒍᑦ ᑕᕝᕙ ᑕᐃᒪᐃᑦᑑᕗᒍᑦ ᐃᓅᓪᓗᑕ ᐊᔾᔨᐅᓇᑕ ᐃᓚᖕᖑᒍᑦ ᐃᓅᖅᑲᑎᑦᑎᓐᓄᑦ, ᐊᑲᐅᖏᒃᑯᑦ ᐊᑲᐅᖕᖏᑦᑐᑎᒍᓪᓗ, ᐱᓪᓗᓇᖅᑐᒃᑯᑦ ᖁᕕᐊᓇᖅᑐᒃᑯᓪᓗ. ᐃᑉᐱᓐᓂᐊᓕᕐᓂᐊᐸᓪᓚᐃᔭᑎᑦ ᑖᓐᓇ ᐅᖃᓕᒫᓕᕈᕕᐅᒃ.

I met Barbara this summer in July 2011, at the home of my grandmother, Elisapee Ishulutak. When I met her she was trying very hard to speak to me in Inuktitut, and I was so proud of her that she was trying to speak our language. I was more surprised to see that she was writing in Inuktitut syllabics, and even using the finals correctly. Then I started to ask her how she learned to write in Inuktitut. We got along really well; it felt like I had known her for a long time. And she was asking me how to pronounce the words properly in Inuktitut. She learned them right away, a smart woman who wanted to learn our language. That is very important to me. My language is how I speak and how I express my feelings and my thoughts.

This book you are going to read is going to make you imagine the North. It felt like I was there, that I left my body and became a part of those people, especially when they were seal hunting. For me I enjoy seal hunting, but sometimes it takes a long time to catch one. Sometimes I get nervous because the men drive the boats very fast and then slow down very quickly. When you read this book you are going to understand more. You might even ᑕᕆᔭᖅᑑᔮᕐᓂᐊᖅᑐᑎᑦ *tarrijaqtuujaarniaqtutit*, feel like you are watching a movie, even though these are short pieces. It makes me so proud of being alive and of my Inukness. This is how we live as Inuit; we are different in some ways from other cultures, through both happiness and hard times. I think you might be touched by this book.

Myna Ishulutak
Iqaluit, Nunavut

Myna Ishulutak teaches Inuktitut at Pirurvik Centre in Iqaluit, and is co-owner of Tajarniit Productions, a film company focusing on Inuit cultural documentaries and Inuktitut language film productions.

ᐸᵖᓂᖅᑑᖅ

*Panniqtuuq**

Getting There

3-hour
flight due north
from Ottawa
to ᐃᖃᓗᐃᑦ *Iqaluit*
1-hour connecting
flight to Pangnirtung

I feel like
Parry and
Franklin
preparing
for the Northwest
Passage

camping gear
for the Arctic
50 pounds of
dry food
textbooks on ᐃᓄᐃᑦ *Inuit*
culture and history

we are 16 students
4 instructors
and the coordinator
of the program
called
the terminator!

I'm on this
adventure to
the North
people ask
why the North
why the Arctic

I want to
learn
ᐃᓄᒃᑎᑐᑦ *Inuktitut*
get my tongue
around the
ancient sounds

I want to know
the beginnings
of this country
taste
the beginnings
of this land

this land
of rock
and ice
land of the caribou
the whale
the polar bear

I want to enter
the womb
of this country
I want
to be
this land

Setting Up

we set up our tents
high on the hill above town

where whitewashed rocks
spell out in huge letters

ᑐᖖᒐᓱᒋᑦ ᐸᓐᓂᖅᑑᒥ
*tunngasugit panniqtuumi**

some of the young men
give us a hand

they bomb up the hill
on their ATVs

and help carry
our extra gear

we hunt for the
perfect spot

not on the soggy
parts of the tundra

a spot that is dry
where water can't collect

I find a good spot
Silasie helps me with my tent

* welcome to Pangnirtung

19

I put rocks around the perimeter
and inside each corner

this is to secure the tent
from the arctic winds

at night I use a bandana
to shield my eyes from the light

a mummy sleeping bag
keeps me warm

in the rain
there are many rhythms

tiny pinpricks
of a light shower

the crackle and pop of a campfire
from the bigger drops

pounding fists
in a torrential storm

I don't want to miss
a single sound

at night my body
sinks into the ground

I sleep soundly
in this cocoon of earth

in the morning I shake off
the bits of dirt

and emerge into the delicious
crisp air

Pangnirtung Fiord

in the distance
sheer rock

clouds floating
between peaks

misty towards
the inner fiord

cool arctic
winds blow

towards the
mountainside

the tundra crawls
between crevices

tiny wildflowers
sprout at my feet

I look out to
the fiord

watching the water
ripple in the wind

the receding tide
leaves a rocky bed

the sky wide open
clouds rolling in and out

the sunlight
always visible

the tundra eagerly soaking
up this midnight sun

it lives for these
months of light

glacial streams
trickle through the tundra

at times a
gushing waterfall

huge boulders
perch

halfway down
the mountainside

how did they
land there

how can they remain
almost in mid-air

the ground is
awash in colour

yellow flowers
delicate stems and leaves

purple buds
ready to burst

the tiny white petals
of Labrador tea

the rocks are the
children's playground

the children are so
sure on their feet

they get soaked
in the soggy tundra

and are covered in
moss and lichens

the fiord is
a perfect picture

the low-hung clouds
sit on the water

the mist lies
over the mountains

the rocks are
the landscape

the tundra its
mossy cloak

Polar Bear

second day
in Pang

a polar bear
sighting

we hear
many stories

ghostly
predator

stealth
hunter

stalking
its prey

silently
watching

silently
calculating

the perfect
attack

living on
the rocks

swimming
the ocean

it smells
its prey

from
afar

it is
king

of the terrestrial
beasts

for the
△⎯ᴑ△ᶜ *Inuit*

the revered
ᴑ⎯ᴑˢᵇ *nanuq*

they
tell us

as we climb
the mountain

to sleep
at night

watch your back!

St. Luke's Anglican Church

a stone holds
the door shut from
the arctic winds
I roll the stone aside
and enter

blue carpet
like the sea
covers the floor
solid oak pews
along each side

sheer white chiffon
curtains cover
the windows
a shiny bronze cross
on the altar

this little church
in Pang
reminds me of
the church
of my childhood

going to church
with my mother
feeling the sensation
of her fur coat
secretly touching it

holding her hands
warm strong hands
with long fingers and
her beautiful antique
wedding ring

I sit at the organ
the Anglican minister
in Pang
has asked me to play the music
for church service

I practice the hymns
she has selected
the melodies are familiar
the words all in
ᐃᓄᒃᑎᑐᑦ *Inuktitut*

on Sunday I arrive early
to go over the hymns
one more time
people start arriving and
glance in my direction

Looie begins the service
the choir enters
their flowing robes
softly swaying as they make
their way to the front of the church

I play too quickly
and have to concentrate
to catch their rhythm
match their tempo
I relax and ease into the music

after the service
one of the choir members
shakes my hand warmly
and tells me I did
a good job

ᖁᔭᓐᓇᒦᒃ *qujannamiik!*
ᐃᓛᓕ *ilaali*

ᓄᓇᕗᑦ ᐅᓪᓗᖓ *Nunavut ullunga*

July 9th
the town is celebrating
ᓄᓇᕗᑦ *Nunavut* Day
with a big feast

at 6 o'clock
we all gather
together
in the hamlet centre

chairs are set up
along the sides for the elders
the place is packed with
families and children

the children
want to play with us
they are curious
about the ᖃᑦᓗᓈᑦ *qallunaat**

big pieces of cardboard
cover the floor
the elders tear off small pieces
I do the same

the hunters come
and empty big boxes
of raw caribou and seal
onto the cardboard

*people down south

we are wide-eyed
looking at the big
chunks of raw meat
and the cut-open seal

Looie is wearing
a beautiful yellow parka
she prays over the food
in her deep baritone voice

the prayers are in ᐃᓄᒃᑎᑐᑦ *Inuktitut*
everyone's head is bowed
except for the little children
still playing

the pieces of cardboard
are our plates
I get a small piece
of frozen raw caribou

the women cut the meat
with the ᐅᓗ *ulu*
a women's knife
and a young mother helps me

I take my first bite
tentative at first
the caribou is frozen
it has a grainy texture

but it is delicious
it tastes like a
very raw steak
and a bit chewy

I try the blubber
it is tasty too
they say the blubber
keeps you warm

I try the seal
it is not frozen
it has a stronger taste
and is very bloody

our fingers are covered
in blood
we are not so adept at eating
the raw meat

we take pictures of
one another
this is so new for us
but our hosts are pleased

the community leaders
come and take
pictures
with us too

this is an ancient
tradition
sharing the bounty
of the hunt

sharing the food with
all the community
sharing the food
in celebration

we have been welcomed
into the community
we have participated
in the feast

ᐃᓅᓯᖅ *Inuusiq*

ᐃᓅᓯᖅ *Inuusiq*
oldest member
in the community

treasure of
mottled skin
phlegmy voice

treasure of
sunken jowls
cloudy vision

treasure of
memory
endless stories

he tells us
about
times past

our people lived
on the land
ᓄᓇᒥ *nunami*

we hunted to
survive
the hunt fed and clothed us

we had to
understand
the animals

how they
moved through
the land

we kept track
of time
by the stars

the northern lights
predicted
the winds

blowing snow
on
foot prints

guided us
back
to camp

the dogs
were
our companions

they pulled the sleds
so necessary
for the hunt

ᓇᑦᑎᖅ *nattiq*
ᑐᑐ *tuttu*
ᐊᒫᕈᖅ *amaruq*

the seal
the caribou
the fox

the dogs kept us
from danger
from the cold

he talks about
climate change
its effect on the North

that what the scientists know
cannot compare
with △ₒ△ᶜ *Inuit* knowledge

he finishes his talk
with stories
of mermaids

how they can
breathe under
water

how they take the children
and put them in
their ◁L▷∩ *amauti**

he is a treasure of
wisdom
a treasure to the community

*△ₒ△ᶜ *Inuit* baby carrier

Conversation with Looie

one evening Gabby
and I visit Looie

we are sitting in
her living room

the big bay window
overlooking the fiord

we ask her about
Pangnirtung

in the 50's and 60's the
△ ᴅ△ᶜ *Inuit* were forced off the land

they were taken to live
in established communities

to ensure they
would not leave

the RCMP killed
their dogs

their dogs were
their means of survival

they were told
the dogs were sick

Looie was just a child
at the time of the catastrophe

she tells us it
broke her parents

we ask her if Pang
feels like home

this will never feel like home
the land is home

after 50 years
the trauma of being forced off the land

has not healed

ᐸᓚᐅᒐᖅ *palaugaaq*

ᐸᓚᐅᒐᖅ *palaugaaq*
the ᐃᓄᒃᑎᑐᑦ *Inuktitut* word for bannock

delicious doughy white bread
cooked in a skillet on the stove top

Oleepika comes to teach us
how to make this carb-rich delight

we have fun in the kitchen
getting our hands into the dough

who invented this simple bread
they say it was the Scots

that even Queen Victoria
enjoyed it with her tea!

when supply boats come to Pang
they must carry large supplies of flour

oil and baking powder
the main ingredients for this bread

no need for yeast
or a perfect baking oven

humble doughy bannock
warm off the stove top

eaten with a slab
of peanut butter or jam

we eat bannock
almost every day

all this delicious doughy bread
is giving us doughy bellies

we call it our ᐸᑕᐅᓕᖅ *palaugaaq* bellies
like carrying a little loaf of bread above our belts

ᑐᖃᒥ

*nunami**

* on the land

Stopping for Lunch

we are a convoy
of fishing boats
heading out
on the ocean

a 6-hour boat ride
ahead of us
from Pangnirtung Fiord
into Cumberland Sound

the day is
perfectly clear
but it is cold
on the water

we are bundled in
all our clothes
double layers
of everything

in the fiord the mountains
rush down to the shore
a skirt of rock
along the edges

in the sound
we pass giant icebergs
the size of
ocean liners

along the way
we stop for lunch
at Alukie and Noah's
summer cabin

it is a small wooden
structure
built on a level piece of
massive rock

it has a cooking area
and sleeping platforms
stacked high
with bedding

outside the cabin
I lie down on the flat rock
the rock warm
from the sun

there is a makeshift
basketball net
made with
a milk crate

it is wired to a stick
standing on the rock
anchored by boulders
around the base

we try a few
basket shots
and take pictures
of our attempts

Noah calls us for lunch
he has caught a seal
Petelosie cuts us each a rib
and we sit by the water to eat

the meat is tasty
and it warms our bellies
we sit in the sun feasting on seal
sunbathing on the rocks

as we are eating
the tide moves in quickly
we have to board the boats
and continue on our way

stopping for lunch was
an adventure
a perfect picnic
in the North

ᐃᑎᓪᓕᑯᓗ *Itillikulu*

ᐃᑎᓪᓕᑯᓗ *Itillikulu*
this is our
campsite along
Clearwater Fiord

we have arrived
at high tide
so we park the boats
close to shore

we have a lot
of work to do
set up the sleeping tents
get the kitchen tent in order

there is a steep mountain
to one side of our site
and a smaller one
on the other side

ᐃᑎᓪᓕᑯᓗ *Itillikulu* means
narrow crossing
here the hunters would
corral the caribou

the elders tell us
the caribou
have moved away now
because of the wolves

they warn us
not to venture far
and to travel
with others

there is a light rain
as we are setting up
the terminator organizes
a warm meal for everyone

soon many are
heading to their tents
to get some sleep
after the long day

but some of us are
too excited to sleep
someone suggests
climbing the mountain

it is after midnight
but in mid-July
the evening sky
is still full of light

let's go
we whisper to one another
and head out over the tundra
to the base of the mountain

Gabby and Katie are
so light on their feet
soon they are up the mountain
and out of sight

I stop halfway up on
a mossy ledge
and decide to wait
till they come back down

I take in the view of the ocean
and our campsite below
the sky is a light purple colour
from the partial sunset

the mountains cast a shadow
over our site
everything completely still
in the early morning hour

suddenly I understand
the ascetics
who lived on mountainsides
their entire lives

I never knew
this beauty existed
nobody ever told me about
the beauty of the North

back south
when people ask me
about the Arctic
I will tell them about this

The Sewing Tent

we have brought
seal skins with us on
the camping trip

the woman are going
to teach us how to make
seal skin mitts

we spend hours
and hours
in the sewing tent

the women teach
us songs
in ᐃᓄᖅᑎᑐᑦ *Inuktitut*

we hear their laughter all day
they tease us
good-naturedly

it is difficult to get
the needle
through the tough leather

Oleepa tells me
my stitches
are too far apart

she looks at one seam that
has taken me ages to sew
ᐋᒡᒪ *aagga* no!

she rips the whole seam apart
and with a big smile tells
me to try again

after three days in the sewing tent
and more than
20 hours of work

I finally complete my mitts
I put them on
and hold them up

everyone starts
applauding
and clapping

I know I will care for
these mittens
with my life

every time I wear them
I will be in
the sewing tent!

My Joke

on an afternoon
excursion
we pass beautiful
mountains
I ask Alukie
the word
for mountain
in ᐃᓄᒃᑎᑐᑦ *Inuktitut*

ᖃᖅᑲᖅ *qaqqaq*
it makes me think of
ᑯᑯ *kuku*
the word for chocolate
we have fun
saying
the double
consonants

I add ᓰᓯ *siisi*
the word for cheese
and Alukie adds the word
ᐊᒫᒪ *amaama*
I want a baby bottle!
it is silly
we both
start laughing

I string all the words
together
ᖃᖅᑲᖅ *qaqqaq*
ᑯᑯ *kuku*
ᓰᓯ *siisi*
ᐊᒫᒪ *amaama*
then jump on the word
ᓴᓗᒐᒪ *sallugama* just joking!

Alukie
bursts into laughter
she loves the
punch line
I have created a joke
in ᐃᓄᒃᑎᑐᑦ *Inuktitut*
she is
proud of me

when we get
to camp
Alukie has me
repeat my joke
to the elders
their faces
crinkle up
with laughter

the children love it too
they start it off
ᖃᖅᑲᖅ *qaqqaq*
ᑯᑯ *kuku*
ᓯᓯ *siisi*
ᐊᒪᒪ *amaama*
then I have to jump
on the punch line ᓴᓪᓗᒐᒪ *sallugama*!

I become famous
for my joke
the elders and the children
ask me to say it
over and over again
they burst
into laughter
every time!

The Seal Hunt

the hunt excites
me
I'm in the boat
bobbing
on the water

ancient
mountains
press to
the water's
edge

the ocean a
deep turquoise
it almost
appears
warm

I imagine diving
into the water
being suffocated
by the shocking
cold

I am drawn
into the space below
with Sedna
goddess of
the sea mammals

a seal comes
and wraps me
in her skin
and I become
her seal pup

I live in this
world
a full-grown seal
with glistening coat
and big brown eyes

I play with the
hunters
know the hunters
understand the
hunters

their need is
great
they need my
flesh
they need my fur

I am willing
to offer them
my body but
first we
must play

I sense the hunters
approach
I can hear
them
from afar

first I rise above
the surface and take a
peek
then dart back
beneath their boat

I rise again
ᐃᒃᑲ ᓇᑦᑎᖅ *ikka nattiq!*
over there
seal!
the game is on

the hunters are
excited
I can hear it
in their
voices

ᐃᒃᑲ *ikka*
ᓇᑦᑎᖅ *nattiq!*
I can
see it
in their eyes

we play
for hours
from one side
of the boat
to the other

Pop!
this time
I let them win
they take my body
they spill my blood

I enter
the spirit world
and return to the
sea goddess
she holds me in her arms

in time
my spirit
enters the body
of a newborn
pup

and
I am back with
my playmates
chasing one another
over the ocean

ᐃᓄᐃᑦ ᐱᕈᖅᓴᐃᔾᔪᓯᖓ *Inuit piruqsaijjusinga**

we stop
in a little
cove
to do some
fishing

Alukie and I stand on
the rocks by the shore
she shows me
how to cast
the line

in the crystal
clear water
you can see the fish
swimming right
up to the lure

Alukie gets so
excited
ᐅᕝᕙ ᐅᕝᕙ *uvva uvva!*
right there
right there!

I get a
few bites
but can't
snag
a thing

* ᐃᓄᐃᑦ *Inuit* parenting

Aidan
Alukie and Noah's
12-year-old son
is fishing on a boulder
right beside us

all of a sudden
there is a shout
from Aidan
he has caught his line
in some seaweed

he can't get it out
he pulls
and pulls
suddenly his fishing rod
snaps in two

he lets out a holler
throws his broken
rod down
and starts to kick
the rocks

he buries his face
in his hands
and sits
on the ground
in tears

Alukie just
lets him be
she doesn't
say
a word

Noah has been
observing
everything
from the
boat

soon we get
ready
to head back
to our
campsite

I wait to see
if Noah will
say anything
to Aidan
not a word

down south
the child
would be reprimanded
for making
a fuss

heading back to camp
Aidan is quiet but
soon he is himself again
with a big grin
on his face

I wonder about
this style of parenting
where there is
no fear
of a child's emotions

ᐃᑦ ᓗᑯᓗ *illukulu*

ᐃᑦ ᓗᑯᓗ *illukulu*
ᐃᑦ ᓗᑯᓗ *illukulu*
cousin
I have been adopted
by Alukie

I go out in Alukie
and Noah's
boat every day
when we are
on the land

Alukie
and Noah
teach us
about
the hunt

Noah is a man
of few words
but
he is always
teaching us

I watch as
he looks
for the seal
as he scans
the ocean surface

I watch as
he takes aim
from the boat
on the bumpy
water

sometimes Alukie
and I duck under
the bow of the boat
into the
sleeping area

it is cozy
and warm from
the heat
of the
Coleman stove

there is always
tea brewing
to warm up
from the cold
on the water

Alukie and I
take a break
and lie down
on the
piled blankets

she teaches me
rhyming songs and
clapping games
in ᐃᓄᒃᑎᑐᑦ *Inuktitut*
we are like schoolgirls

she tells me
about her relationship
with Noah
what a wonderful
husband and father he is

she tells me
how he loves to look
at her
especially when
she has no makeup on

I tell Alukie
how happy I am for her
she teaches me
the words in ᐃᓄᒃᑎᑐᑦ *Inuktitut*
ᖁᕕᐊᒋᒋᒃᑭᑦ *quviagigikkit*

she also teaches me
the word for cousin
she tells me ᐃᓪᓗᑯᓗᒌᓕᖅᑐᒍᒃ
illukulugiiliqtuguk
we are now cousins!

I am touched by her affection
I feel responsible
to her now
I am responsible
for my ᐃᓪᓗᑯᓗ *illukulu*

Nadia

Noah takes Nadia
his teenage daughter
and her cousin Sheema
out night hunting
Marion and I are
invited along

it is a beautiful evening
the water is so still
it is like glass
the sun partially
hidden by the mountains
along the fiord

Nadia and Sheema
are at the bow
of the boat
scanning the water
we are always
looking for seal

Nadia spots one
ᐄᑉᐃ *ikka*!
Noah turns the boat
and guns the motor
we race towards
the spot

Noah cuts the motor
and we wait for the
seal to rise again
to the surface
we chase it for a while
then lose its trail

Nadia has a little crush
on one of the students
from Québec
she wants to know how
to say you are handsome
in French

Marion teaches her.
tu es très beau
Nadia practises
with Sheema
tu es très beau
tu es très beau

after a while
the girls
go under the bow
of the boat
to hang out
in the sleeping area

we continue to look
for seal
but no
luck this night
and we head back
to camp

when we get back
I tell Gilbert
Nadia has something
to tell him
but she is too shy
and runs away

later that night
when I'm playing cards
with the children
Nadia asks me how
to say the phrase again
tu es très beau

Cleaning the Seal

Noah is teaching Gilbert and Tee
how to clean the seal

the seal is laid out on
the rocks close to shore

Noah pours fresh water
into the seal's mouth

he explains this is an ancient custom
to alleviate the seal's thirst

Noah sharpens his knife
and skins the seal

he shows Gilbert and Tee
how to cut beneath the layer of fat

the layer of fat
has to be perfect

not too thick
not too thin

the heart and choice pieces
of meat are cut away

the ribs are cut
into separate pieces

the seal is going to be cooked
in a stew called ᐅᔾᔪᖅ *uujuq*

the seal will feed all the camp
the meat is put into huge pots

and is cooked outside
on the Coleman stoves

when the meat is ready to eat
there is a loud announcement

all the camp gathers together
Jayco says prayers over the food

the children and elders line up
the elders get the choice pieces of meat

we sit on the rocks to have our feast
I find a spot beside Tauki

Tauki is one of the elders
she has been helping us in the sewing tent

I chat with Tauki
her English is pretty good

she asks if she can borrow my knife
you cannot eat seal without a good knife

the seal meat feeds us
the seal meat nourishes us

for thousands of years
the △ᴅ△ᶜ *Inuit* have relied upon the seal

without the seal
it would be impossible to survive

Joanasie˙

Joanasie
ᐊᑖᑕ *ataata**

teaches us
many things

he takes us to an
ancient ᑐᓂᑦ *Tunit* site

he tells us they were
ancestors of the ᐃᓄᐃᑦ *Inuit*

we see the remains
of their homes

they are made
of rock

the opening to
the houses are tiny

some people believe
the ᑐᓂᑦ *Tunit* were small

but others say
they were giants

they were known
for their hunting abilities

* father, elder

they hunted the whale
from their kayaks

spearing the whale
with the harpoon

in the hunt the ⊃σᶜ *Tunit*
were covered in blood

but they persisted until
they landed their prey

Joanasie teaches us
about the Δ⸑ᐤᑉᖰᑉ *inuksuk*

how they were guides
for navigation

pointing out caribou
hunting grounds

where to find
abundant fish

the Δ⸑ᐤᑉᖰᑉ *inuksuk* pointed
the direction home

they had meaning and
were read by the hunters

Joanasie teaches us
about shamans

how they can be under
water with the animals

their abilities
to appease the sea goddess

their powers in the human world
and the animal world

he tells us you can't be told
you are a shaman

you must discover
it for yourself

on the land
he tells us many stories

he shares the abundance
of his knowledge

Games

Noah and Alukie
organize games at night

we have a
scavenger hunt

4 feathers
4 wild berries

4 rocks and as many
mosquitoes as possible

no problem
ᑭᑐᕆᐊᖅᐸᓗᐃᑦ *kitturiaqpaaluit!*

we are living with
tons of mosquitoes!

I find the feathers
wild berries and rocks

I know there are swarms
of mosquitoes in our tent

I race off to our tent
and catch 12

I run back to the finish line
thinking I'm going to win

Alukie's sister Rosie
wins with 82!

the hunters are superior
even with mosquitoes

another game is a race with
string and an empty pop can

a piece of string is tied
to the back of our pants

a nail is tied to
the end of the string

we have to hook the nail
into the opening of the pop can

then run to
the finish line

we cannot use
our hands

if the can falls off
we have to start again

I am hopeless
at hooking the can

Rosie wins
this one too

we watch the men
compete

the final race is between
Noah and Gilbert

Noah crosses the
finish line

before Gilbert can
even hook his can

we are no match
for our hosts!

Hair Washing

one morning
Alukie takes
my hand
and says she's going
to wash my hair

we walk over
to the little stream
that flows down
the mountain
and empties into the fiord

Alukie finds a spot
where the water has pooled
I hunch down and dip
my head into the water
it is freezing

Alukie quickly shampoos
and rinses my mop of hair
I walk back to the campsite
with a towel wrapped
around my head

the others ask us
to wash their hair too
we have started a craze
we hold hands
as we walk to the pool

this is something
women love to do
walk hand in hand
women are very physical
in their affection

maybe from all the things
they do with their hands
bathing the babies
soothing a sick child
caressing a lover

in the North
women's hands
do the tasks of men too
they hunt the seal
raise the tents

all hands are joined in
the work of the community
all hands are joined
in taking care of
one another

it is not a burden
to take care of the children
take care of the elders
it is life itself
to care for the community

the simple act
of washing one another's hair
not being locked
in isolated lives
separated from one another

the △ᗡ△ᶜ *Inuit* didn't need
any foreign religion
to come and teach them
how to share with one another
care for one another

they have known this
for thousands of years

Last Night in ᐃᑎᓪᓕᑯᓗ *Itillikulu*

we are leaving the next day
at high tide
we don't want to leave
and imagine staying

we are sitting on the beach
sipping chai tea Sarra has made
it is deliciously
sweet and warm

it is close to midnight
someone suggests climbing
the mountain
one last time

it is a beautiful night
the sun is setting
there is no wind
this time I make it to the top

we collect armfuls of fireweed
Henry makes a fire
we sit around telling stories
and singing in ᐃᓄᒃᑎᑐᑦ *Inuktitut*

we make an ᐃᓄᒃᓱᒃ *inuksuk*
on the highest point
it stands silhouetted against
the clear night sky

as the sun is rising
we make our way
down the mountain
to the sleeping camp below

it is just a few hours
before we leave
I walk over to
the stream that feeds the fiord

I wash my face in the ice cold water
and look up at the day moon
hovering just
above the horizon

ᐅᑎᕆᓂᖅ ᐸᓐᓂᖅᑑᒧᑦ

*utirniq panniqtuumut**

* back in Pangnirtung

Back in Pang

in town
people ask about
our camping trip
they ask about the mosquitoes

ᑭᑐᓂᐊᖅᐸ̇ᓗᐃᑦ *kitturiaqpaaluit!*
they always chuckle
when we say
tons of mosquitoes!

we are back at work
I'm helping Looie
prepare for the
Healing of the Land

we practise the songs
for the celebration
I'm playing keyboards
for the band

on breaks I head downtown
to one of the local stores
these are the spots
to hang out in Pang

there are 3
the Northern
the Co-op
and the convenience store

the Northern is
a grocery store
plus clothes and
some furniture

it is run by a company
out of Winnipeg
someone is making a profit
the prices are sky high

at the Co-op the prices
are still high
but the profits go back
into the community

at the Co-op I like to sit on
the ledge by the check-out counter
and watch the people
coming in and out

or grab a coffee
and stand outside
on the steps
of the Co-op

I say hi to the people
coming and going
and practice my
ᐃᓄᒃᑎᑐᑦ *Inuktitut*

ᖃᓄᐃᑉᐱᑦ *qanuippit?*
ᖃᓄᐃᙱᑦᑐᖓ *qanuinngittunga*
ᐃᕝᕕᓪᓕ *ivvilli?*
ᖃᓄᐃᙱᑦᑐᖓ *qanuinngittunga*

just like down south
at the outdoor cafés
people love to watch
other people going by

for so many months we are
bundled up in our homes
so hanging out in the summer
is such a pleasure

for a moment
all is well in the world
when you stop and watch
the world go by

Healing of the Land

a preacher from Fiji
is coming to celebrate
the Healing of the Land

they have a similar service
in Fiji to heal the rifts
between the different tribes

it is Thursday evening
the first night of the service
it will last over 4 days

I am with Looie when
she finds out one of the elders
has passed away

she tells me there will be no service
when there is a passing
everything shuts down

everyone is talking
in ᐃᓄᒃᑎᑐᑦ *Inuktitut*
Mary translates for me

it is Tauki who has passed away
we were with her just
a few days ago

she was with us on the land
she taught us how to sew our mittens
I run to tell the other students

everyone is silent
we're not prepared
for this kind of news

the Healing of the Land
resumes the following day
there is a huge turnout

people comfort
one another
over the recent loss

the prayers last through
the night
the children sit and play

no-one is worried
about the noise
they make

it rains
throughout
the weekend

on the last evening
of service
the sun comes out

there is a rainbow
all the children run
outside to look

in the closing prayers
to the community
Looie prays for blessings

as we leave the service
she tells us
angels will escort us home

that night
is the easiest climb
up the mountain

August Long Weekend

we head out on the water
for the day

as we are leaving the harbour
two speed boats rush by

there is a transmission
over the CB radio

there is a flurry of chatter
in ᐃᓄᒃᑎᑐᑦ *Inuktitut*

all I can catch is someone
on the speed boat is receiving CPR

and Lootie has Noah's boat
Noah is the lead hunter in the community

he is young and strong
all must be fine

            *   *   *

as we enter Cumberland Sound
we pass a giant iceberg

our boat is small enough
so we get quite close

it is a floating ice mountain
chilling the surrounding air

all of a sudden Petelosie
spots a bowhead whale

there are about four of them
in the distance

we cut the motor and listen to them
blowing as they rise to the surface

they look like
mythical creatures

their huge grey bodies
lifting out of the water

*   *   *

we are on our way
to Petelosie's summer cabin

there are thick clouds ahead of us
they touch the surface of the water

soon we enter into complete fog
I wonder how Petelo can navigate the boat

soon the shore and the cabin
emerge from the mist

we park the boat
and pile inside the cabin

Petelo lights the Coleman stove
and makes a big pot of tea

his mother has sent along
fresh ᐸᑕᐅᓕᖅ *palaugaaq*

we feast on ᐸᑕᐅᓕᖅ *palaugaaq*
and jam

we relax at the cabin for a while
then head back out on the water

suddenly Petelo yells out
polar bear!

it is just ahead of us
it is swimming towards the shore

we are so close
we can hear it breathing

we follow the bear to the shore
he clambers onto the rocks

he shakes off the frigid water
and stares back at us

we are snapping pictures
as fast as we can

the bear runs up the side of the cliff
and disappears over the rocks

we look at one another speechless
we start to hoot and holler

Corina is dancing on the nose of the boat
Petelo has a grin from ear to ear

*　　　*　　　*

now that we are into August
there is less light at night

we drive home
in semi-darkness

as we enter Pangnirtung fiord
we run out of fuel

Petelo uses the naphtha gas from
the Coleman stove to get us home

it is low tide
we cannot enter the harbour

Petelo drops us off and
we hike across the sandy bed

in the distance I can see
Gilbert's silhouette

an uneasy thought arises
I race towards the shore

Gilbert tells us we have
to come to the school

he won't explain
what has happened

I meet Silasie along the way
he gives me a hug

he is shaking
I ask him what's wrong

Noah is gone
what

Noah is gone
he drowned this afternoon

I drop to the ground
it can't be possible

we make it back to the school
everyone is crying

      *   *   *

it is after 2 o'clock in the morning
I can't climb the mountain

I stay at Lucasie's house
his parents are with Alukie

we watch TV until 4 in the morning
I try to sleep for a few hours

at 9 o'clock
I wander back to the school

Wayne is on the steps
he tells me some of the details

Noah and his family were
out on the boat

they began to have
engine problems

Noah was fixing the motor
somehow he fell into the water

the current is very strong
they could not get the boat close to him

they tried to throw him a rope
but he lost strength very quickly

you can only last a very short time
in water that cold

the women radioed for help
the emergency boats raced there

they did CPR
but he was already gone

we are all still in shock
I go to see Alukie

when I enter her house
it is full of women

I can hear Alukie crying
in the bedroom

one of the family members
tells her I'm here

she comes out
I give her a hug

there are no words
to say

there are no words
for this sorrow

Tauki's Funeral

it is a sad time in Pang
Tauki's funeral is on Wednesday

family members from all over the North
have flown in for the funeral

I arrive at the church early
they have told us the church will be packed

just before the service begins
my friend Mary slips in beside me

Looie welcomes us
and begins the service

at one point Looie invites people
to come up and speak about Tauki

Mary turns to me and asks
if I would like to say something

all the service is in ᐃᓄᒃᑎᑐᑦ *Inuktitut*
she says she will translate for me

I am shy to step forward
but make myself go up to the front

thank you Tauki
ᖁᔭᓐᓇᒦᒃ *qujannamiik*

you were so sweet
so kind to all the students

you were so patient
teaching us how to sew

thank you Tauki
we love you

that night back at the school
a young man introduces himself

he has come to Pang from Kimmirut
he gives me a big hug

he thanks me for speaking at
his grandmother's funeral

Noah's Funeral

Noah's funeral is the next day
it is at the school

we spend the morning setting up the gym
we set up over 400 chairs

Looie asks if I'll play the music
Noah's sisters have picked out the hymns

soon people start arriving
the gym fills up quickly

there is lamenting
from every corner

I start playing the opening hymn
Alukie and the children arrive

the wailing and lamenting
reach the heavens

Looie begins
the opening prayers

she asks the men who performed CPR
on Noah to come to the front

6 burly men come
forward to the altar

they form a circle with their
arms around one another

Looie prays over them
tears stream down their faces

lament breaks out
throughout the congregation

Looie asks if anyone would like
to say a few words

many people come forward
to thank Noah and his family

Gilbert and Tee go up
together to speak

they thank Noah for teaching them
how to clean the seal

how to give the seal
fresh water to drink

they thank Alukie
and the children

the service continues
finally it is the closing hymn

the men come forward to carry
out the coffin

the lamenting is almost
too much to bear

the people slowly exit and we walk
to the cemetery by the water

the family watch as the men
from the community take turns

shovelling dirt onto
the grave

a light rain
muffles the sounds

Noah Metuq

Noah
loving father
husband
friend

premier hunter
provider
mentor to
the young

sovereign of
the fishing boat
the tides
the nets

sovereign
of the animals
on the water
on the land

the caribou
the seal
the whale
the fox

sovereign
of the
community's
heart

he is gone
he has been called
to the hidden
world

they longed
for him to be
sovereign
in their world

they needed
someone
to teach them how
to hunt

how to
hunt
and clean
the seal

how to catch
the char
from the frozen
sea

how to herd
and stalk
the swift
caribou

the people of
the hidden world
pleaded
with the gods

we have seen
what Noah can do
his strength
his power

please give us
this hunter
we are lost without
a provider

the lords of
the hidden
world
convened

what shall
we do
our people
are hungry

they have been
without
a premier hunter
for so long

we can take this hunter
from the living
and give him
to our people

one lord opposed
what about his family
his wife
his children

but the many insisted
we must bring
Noah
to our world

we will
weep
with the people
of the living

our lament
will echo
through the mountains
over the seas

Noah will save
our world
he will understand
the sacrifice

his spirit
will be free
to pass through both
our worlds

his spirit
will travel every night
into the dreams of his
loved ones

his spirit
will be with
the animals
with
the hunt

his spirit will lie
on the water
and upon
our hearts

he will be sovereign
of both our worlds

Last Day in Pang

spending the day
saying goodbye to friends

I walk over to the Angmarlik Centre
to say goodbye to Kelly

I'm exhausted
from the past few days

and fall asleep
in a corner of the museum

later I make my way
to Alukie's house

her place is filled with relatives
people from the community

there are tons of kids
I take them outside to play soccer

Alukie has to go out for a while
and a group of us clean her house

when Alukie comes back
we say our goodbyes

I invite her to come visit me
in Toronto

we hug each other and I give her
one last kiss

I drop by Mary's house
but she's not home

I ask her husband
to say goodbye for me

I spend the evening with Evie
Silasie's grandmother

she shows me
her prayer book

we read the prayers together
in ᐃᓄᒃᑎᑐᑦ *Inuktitut*

we look out her window
over the Pangnirtung Fiord

she whispers to me
ᐱᐅᔪᖅ ᐹᓗᒃ *piujuqpaaluk*!

it is so
beautiful!

ᑕᑯᓐᖑᔪᑦ *takulaarivugut*

we pack up our tents and
head down the mountain one last time

Joanasie and Henry arrive with trucks
to take the luggage to the airport

the airport is just behind the school
so we walk over together

our group fills up
the whole airport building

lots of kids have run over
to say goodbye

when the flight to ᐃᖃᓗᐃᑦ *Iqaluit* is announced
a huge roar goes up in the crowd

there are wild hugs and kisses
we run out the door and board the plane

as the plane taxis to the end of the runway
the children follow us running alongside the fence

looking out my tiny window
I can see the children wildly waving their arms

I wave back
and burst into tears

this is only a temporary
goodbye

when people part in the North
they say ᑕᑯᓚᕆᕗᒍᑦ *takulaarivugut*

we will see each other again

ᐃᓄᐃᑦ ᑎᑎᕋᐅᓯᖏᑦ *Inuit titirausingit*

ᐃ	i	ᐅ	u	ᐊ	a		
ᐱ	pi	ᐳ	pu	ᐸ	pa	ᑉ	p
ᑎ	ti	ᑐ	tu	ᑕ	ta	ᑦ	t
ᑭ	ki	ᑯ	ku	ᑲ	ka	ᒃ	k
ᒋ	gi	ᒍ	gu	ᒐ	ga	ᒡ	g
ᒥ	mi	ᒧ	mu	ᒪ	ma	ᒻ	m
ᓂ	ni	ᓄ	nu	ᓇ	na	ᓐ	n
ᓯ	si	ᓱ	su	ᓴ	sa	ᔅ	s
ᓕ	li	ᓗ	lu	ᓚ	la	ᓪ	l
ᔨ	ji	ᔪ	ju	ᔭ	ja	ᔾ	j
ᕕ	vi	ᕗ	vu	ᕙ	va	ᕝ	v
ᕆ	ri	ᕈ	ru	ᕋ	ra	ᕐ	r
ᖀ	qi	ᖁ	qu	ᖃ	qa	ᖅ	q
ᖏ	ngi	ᖑ	ngu	ᖓ	nga	ᖕ	ng
ᖠ	łi	ᖢ	łu	ᖤ	ła	ᖦ	ł

Acknowledgements

There are many people to thank. First I would like to thank Alana Johns and Saila Michael, my Inuktitut instructors at the University of Toronto, for encouraging me to sign up for the Pangnirtung program. A big thank you goes to Peter Kulchyski from the University of Manitoba, director of the summer program in Pang. Over the years Peter has developed many friendships within the Inuit community, and is able to offer students a unique and profound experience. I am very grateful to Peter and to all the instructional team for the superlative program they provided. I would also like to thank Lindsay Terry, coordinator of the program, and all the other participants.

There are not enough words to thank our Inuit hosts. Their patience and guidance were endless. They protected us, fed us, taught us, extended their friendship and affection to each member of the group. It was truly humbling to experience such deep generosity.

I would also like to thank the publishers at Quattro Books for believing this was an important story to tell, and my editors Luciano Iacobelli and Allan Briesmaster for their thoughtful suggestions throughout the process.

I would like to extend my deepest gratitude to Myna Ishulutak who took time to read through the manuscript and guide me with the Inuktitut spellings, and who generously offered to write the introduction. This book could not have been published without her help.

And finally I would like to give special thanks to my partner Len Steel, for his artistic collaboration and unending support and encouragement.

Many thanks to all of you.

ᖃᐅᔨᓴᓕᖅ *qujannamiik!*

Other Quattro Poetry Books

jumping in the asylum by Patrick Friesen
Without Blue by Chris D'Iorio
When the Earth by Lisa Young
And tell tulip the summer by Allan Graubard
Book of Disorders by Luciano Iacobelli
Saugeen by Rob Rolfe
Strong Bread by Giovanna Riccio
Rough Wilderness by Rosemary Aubert
hold the note by Domenico Capilongo
syrinx and systole by Matthew Remski
Sew Him Up by Beatriz Hausner
Psychic Geographies and Other Topics by Gregory Betts
The Sylvia Hotel Poems by George Fetherling
Ten Thousand Miles Between Us by Rocco de Giacomo
A River at Night by Paul Zemokhol
This Is How I Love You by Barbara Landry
Looking at Renaissance Paintings by Caroline Morgan Di Giovanni
The Hawk by Rob Rolfe
My Etruscan Face by Gianna Patriarca
Garden Variety Edited by Lily Contento
MIC CHECK Edited by David Silverberg
Evidence by Samuel Andreyev
Interstellar by Allan Briesmaster